BRAIN TIPS

Simple Yet Sensational Brain-Friendly Strategies for Improving Teaching, Learning, and Parenting

By Dr. Linda Karges-Bone

Author of *Differentiated Pathways of the Brain*, *Breaking Brain Barriers*, *Brain Verse* and *Brain Framing*

Edited by Bonnie Krueger
Cover and Book design by Kati Hufford

Lorenz Educational Press
a Lorenz company
P.O. Box 802
Dayton, OH 45401-0802

www.LorenzEducationalPress.com

TABLE OF CONTENTS

90/1096LE

INTRODUCTION AND IMPLICATIONS

Brain Tips is a book about possibilities and promises. According to Dr. Gerald Edelman in *Bright Air, Brilliant Fire* (Edelman 1992), the human brain's pre-frontal cortex, if smoothed out, is about the size of a linen dinner napkin. If one attempted to count the possible neural connections in this pre-frontal cortex at the rate of 1 per second, it would take 32 MILLION YEARS.

Amazing, but also daunting.

How can teachers better access these neural connections? The eight sections of brain tips can help busy teachers dig more deeply into what matters in the gray matter. *Brain Tips* is simple yet sophisticated, beginning with the teacher's brain and moving through subsequent sections on boys' and girls' brains, the sensory brain, accommodations for differentiation and RTI, creativity and critical thinking, neuro-architecture, and parenting. The latest research is distilled to an elixir that teachers can drink in and work into their teaching.

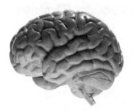

This book is dedicated to Barbara Meeks and Bonnie Krueger, the mother-daughter creative team at Lorenz Educational Press who always see the possibilities of the brain and of the author, and who want to make the mysteries and possibilities of cognitive science available to all teachers.

I dwell in Possibility—
A fairer House than Prose—
More numerous of Windows—
Superior–for Doors
(Dickinson, "I Dwell in Possibility," #657)

SECTION ONE: TEACHER STRESS AND THE BRAIN

According to research in the United States, Great Britain, and Canada, teaching is the most stressful profession. Now, there may be more stressful jobs, such as being an EMT or a coal miner, but a profession is one that requires university training. Teachers are professionals who not only work under enormous stress, but who must concurrently function at a very high level of thinking called

METACOGNITION

Simply put, *metacognition* means "thinking about thinking." It is necessary for teachers to maintain optimum levels of critical thinking and creativity to carry out a variety of tasks, including implementing state and national standards, accommodating the needs of a diverse group of learners, and making up to 3,000 non-trivial educational decisions per day (Danielson 1996).

Use the nine tips in this section to maintain metacognition and reduce stress.

4

Tip #1
Eat More Almonds

Your amygdala turns on when you are under stress. What is an amygdala? This almond-shaped structure triggers the release of the stress hormone cortisol when one is under stress. This can impede your creativity and slow down response time. However, eating almonds is one way to appease this pesky neuro-structure.

Amygdala is the Greek word for "almond." Interestingly, almonds are one of the top brain foods, providing choline, which feeds neurons. An empty cough drop or mint tin is the perfect dose of roasted almonds to nosh on in the classroom. Eating almonds helps you to take a break and refuel the brain at the same time. Teachers need snack time, too! Hit the pause button and recharge your brain with almonds for your amygdala.

Tip #2
Build A Support Network (Carefully)
And Avoid Toxic Teachers

Social capital is essential for maintaining
metacognition. Select and nurture a circle of
friends who positively support your career path.
Avoid toxic teachers!

Teacher "burn-out" is real. In *Beyond Burnout* (Cherniss 1995), Cary Cherniss identified five stressors that contribute to half of all teachers leaving the profession by the end of five years. One of these is a lack of support and the accompanying loneliness of the profession. While seeking out positive support and meaningful interaction, beware of "toxic teachers" who focus on the negative attributes of teaching. These unhappy folks will steal your joy.

Who can you count on to affirm your decision to teach and teach well?

Tip #3
Take Care of Yourself Physically and Emotionally

Or, Put the Oxygen Mask on Yourself First

Maintaining metacognition is physically grueling. Research suggests that the very same personality traits and disposition that draw you into the helping professions will actually turn on you after a time. Putting others first is admirable, but if your energy and resources are so depleted that depression and ill health take hold, then both you and your students lose.

How can teachers maintain their physical edge?

• Regular massage
(often paid for by health insurance as part of chiropractic treatment)

• A Zumba® or dance class
(many gyms give teacher discounts)

• Keeping weekends sacred for family and rest time

Tip #4
Design Your Work Space With the Brain in Mind

Think of yourself as a neuro-architect. Consider the use of space, light, color, water features and plants to stimulate your own serotonin and dopamine levels.

Section six of this resource is devoted to neuro-architecture. Before reading it, gain a sense of awareness about the ways that environment can trigger the release of the stress hormone cortisol by responding to the following statements:

Over the past week, I could not find paperwork or materials that I needed because of clutter in my workspace.

YES   NO

I have clearly defined areas in my classroom that reflect my passions, such as science, the arts, or publishing.

YES   NO

Green plants are part of my classroom design.

YES   NO

Classical music is available on my music player or computer and is routinely used during work time.

YES   NO

I change the configuration of desks and tables at least once per month.

YES   NO

If you have fewer than four YES responses, flip to the neuro-architecture section now (page 53).

Tip #5
Think of Yourself as a Creative Person

You are the most creative force in the classroom universe. Defining yourself as creative is essential to maintaining metacognition. Do what all artists do: Maintain a portfolio.

It is easy to lose sight of the person who, perhaps just a few years earlier, was so eager to create a classroom space and culture that was inviting and invigorating. You might need to do a visualization exercise. For that, you will need a portfolio.

• Pull out some photographs of yourself as a student or first-year teacher. Place these into your portfolio.

• Gather the good notes from children and parents that you have collected. Place these into your portfolio.

• Collect newspaper clippings from your school's archive since you were on staff. You are part of this story; place these into your portfolio.

• Organize the formal class photographs from each year. Count the number of children whom you have impacted. 30 or 300? Let your portfolio document the sheer mass of your creativity.

Tip #6
Regulate Your Emotional Temperature

If you were going to be categorized, would you be a thermometer or a thermostat in the classroom? Your answer matters in regards to metacognition.

According to Tim Elmore, author of *Habitudes* (Elmore 2010), there are two kinds of leaders: thermometers and thermostats. A "thermometer teacher" would be a person who reflects the affective, or emotional, tone and temperature of the students. Anger, anxiety, frustration—all of these negative emotions could potentially trigger dangerous readings in the teacher's brain.

On the other hand, a "thermostat teacher" regulates the classroom, literally and figuratively. This kind of teacher is constant, keeping his or her brain in focus and fearless. In this state, you can influence the environment, using, of course, metacognition.

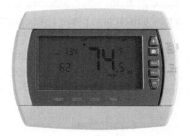

Choose to be a thermostat. Need a reminder? Put up a big, red thermometer as a prompt!

Tip #7
Smile with Your Eyes

You know how people are always saying, "Use your teacher voice"? I've got a new one for you: "Use your teacher eyes."

In an interesting study published in the *Journal of Motivation and Emotion* in 2009, researchers found that individuals who smiled broadly and enthusiastically in yearbook photographs were five times less likely to divorce later in life than their more stoic peers.

So, smile at your children. That is a given. But for metacognition, take it a step further. Make sure the smile is in your eyes, too. We have mirror neurons that reflect emotions. When children see our genuine smiles light up our eyes, the message is clear: "You are welcome here." This sets a tone of good will that pays double dividends in stress reduction: the act of smiling triggers dopamine in your brain, and it also sets the students at ease by releasing more opiates in their own brains. Win-win.

Tip # 8
Become a Morning Person

First recorded in *A Compleat Collection of English Proverbs* by John Ray, the saying "the early bird catcheth the worm" is backed up with current brain research. And, it can help to reduce your stress levels.

Fast forward to 2013: Researchers at Harvard University found that people tend to be more honest in the morning. By the afternoon, participants in the study became emotionally and ethically "weaker," more prone to cheat on tests, and less likely to be able to self-regulate.

What's the lesson for teachers seeking to reduce stress? It is two-fold:

1. Structure your lesson plans to do the most difficult tasks for both yourself and your students before lunchtime.

2. Be aware of the threats of mental fatigue in the afternoon and structure breaks that rejuvenate you and your students.

Tip # 9
Use Dr. Bone's 1-2-3 Strategy

Teachers' stress is real and demands real action in order to achieve balance. That may be easier said than done. We can all benefit from a personal trainer for our brains. After all, people pay a lot of money to have someone in fancy workout gear count out sit ups or jog with them around the block.

Achieve greater balance in your day with this brain coach's 1-2-3 strategy!

Make a point of listening to your students instead of simply responding to their questions. *Active* or *attentive listening*, developed by Dr. Alfred Adler, can create a more peaceful dynamic in your day.

Double-duty or 2-for-1 thinking is ideal for assessments. Use science vocabulary in a writing activity. Pair reading and social studies standards into a single grade.

Make an old-fashioned list and then deconstruct it. This doesn't necessarily mean not doing something. It may mean doing it in a way that leaves you with more time. For example, a friend may want you to attend a fund-raising event. Offer to make a small donation instead.

SECTION TWO: BOY-FRIENDLY BRAIN TIPS

The question of differentiating for boys and girls in the classroom is one of style, not substance. Although some theorists demand a pure, hard-line view on what is called *single gender* or *single sex* differentiation, my take on it is more subtle. I believe that simple gender-friendly accommodations can make a credible difference in the ways that boys and girls learn. Let's consider boys first.

Tip #1
Play with a Brain Ball

Simple props such as a vinyl, inflatable beach ball can be used to keep neurons zipping about the pre-frontal cortex. This activity is boy-friendly because 1) it involves movement, and 2) it demands a verbal response. Try the beach ball prop in two ways:

As a tool of inquiry. Using an inexpensive, inflatable beach ball and a permanent marker, write questions or prompts on each colored stripe. Toss or pass the ball to a child, and invite him to respond to the question or prompt that lands facing him.

As a mini-therapy ball. Using the same method described above, inscribe the stripes of the ball with prompts from the *affective* (relating to moods, feelings, and attitudes), rather than *cognitive* (relating to thinking and understanding), domain of learning. Teachers can write personalized prompts on the stripes of the ball to fit his or her program. Giving voice to one's feelings, positive or negative, is a good way to keep serotonin levels even in the brain. This optimizes brain function.

*For a detailed discussion of how to create and use these brain balls, see *Differentiated Pathways of the Brain* (Karges-Bone 2010).

Tip #2
Use Colored Folders

Research suggests that boys, who are often more visual than auditory learners, may develop better organizational skills when colored folders are used as a teaching and learning strategy.

This is a form of coding and helps to activate neural pathways in the front of the brain. A different color for each subject area or for each kind of task can help active boys to maintain control of their learning.

Folder Color	Subject
Blue	Mathematics
Green	Creative Writing
Orange	Science
Red	Agenda
Yellow	Signed Papers
Purple	Social Studies

Tip #3
Trading Cards for Literacy

Testosterone makes boys naturally competitive, and teachers can use that to their advantage by making "book cards" a hot commodity in the classroom. Research suggests that girls enjoy reading more than boys do. We can change that by pairing books and trading cards that can be 1) collected, 2) traded for prizes, and 3) accumulated to win awards and recognition.

Remember that boys often prefer non-fiction books, so maintain a robust collection of books about natural disasters, animals, heroes, unusual creatures, and a distinct boy-favorite: world records!

READING ZONE
Trading Card

Title: _____

Author: _____

The main character is: _____

_____.

Three great things about this book:

_____.

_____.

_____.

Tip #4
Introduce Balance Ball Chairs

We know that boys like to be active and that often classroom management issues trigger when boys get in trouble for not staying still in their seats. What would happen if you put boys into a seated experience that fits their learning style?

Balance ball chairs are a great solution for active boys. Contrary to what you might fear, boys do not seem to roll around like pinballs in a slot machine once ensconced in these innovative seats. Instead, they must stay still and engage their cores, as well as their brains, in order to stay upright.

Image courtesy of Gaiam, http://www.gaiam.com

Here are some additional tips for using balance ball chairs with boys:

> Put one balance ball chair at each four-person table, and have the boys "earn" time in the chair.

> Rotate the chairs to different parts of the room each day, and surprise the boys with a new seat.

> Consider a single-gender ELA class, which is a weaker area for many boys, and outfit it with balance ball chairs.

Tip #5
Try Toolboxes for Learning

Boys like tools. It is imprinted in most males. Their sense of visual-spatial intelligence is the one area of brain development that is consistently more highly developed than females. Take advantage of this and direct this strength toward two classroom weaknesses:

1. Organization
2. Verbal skills

Take small toolboxes (donated by a local hardware store or PTA) and outfit them with "learning tools," such as highlighting pens, interesting pencils, markers, rulers, a small egg timer, and a stash of blue bandages (see page 20). Put one toolbox in the center of each work group. The idea of using tools to attack a language challenge, such as writing a paragraph or finding the verb in a sentence, triggers boys' competitive sides and their desire to solve problems.

Tip #6
Use Blue Bandages for Reading

More boys than girls are diagnosed with dyslexia, which is, in its purest form, a struggle to read. Of course, this takes many forms, but part of the dyslexic's struggle often stems from:

1. Trouble tracking left to right over text

2. Trouble with focus

3. Trouble with visual discrimination

4. Frustration from all of the above

The "blue bandage" concept comes from my roots as a special education teacher, where we often used blue overlays to help struggling readers. This concept is a modification.

Copy and cut out bandages on blue construction paper. Laminate the bandages. Attach the bandage to a craft stick for easy handling and to keep them from getting lost.

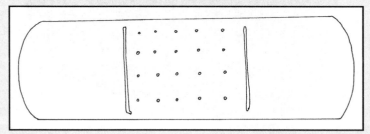

Students use their individual blue bandages to track text, stay focused, and remain calm. The blue color may also be therapeutic; shades of blue can actually slow down one's heart rate, hence "cardiac blue" is a color often used in hospitals.

Tip #7
Engage in Brain-Friendly Reading Activities

This boy-brain tip involves harvesting recycled telephone books and telephones. Yes, the old yellow pages and a variety of archaic handsets can be very helpful to the gender-friendly teacher. Use these found objects to set up an activity titled, "Who Ya Gonna Call? Math Busters!"

1. Divide the boys into pairs or small groups, and give them challenges, such as:

Our teacher's birthday is next week, and we want to order a cake.	Our soccer team needs new shirts with the logo on it.
We want a speaker to come in and talk about careers in the military.	Our pet pig is not eating well. Is there a veterinarian who deals with small farm animals?

2. Students must find the answers in the phone directories and "talk" the answers out on the phones. These steps coordinate right and left brains and demand use of more words. Remember, boys typically use about 6,000 words per day, compared to the 20,000 that girls command.

Why not use the Internet? It's too easy, and there's not enough of a reading challenge.

Tip #8
Buddy Up with Younger Readers

The opposite of anger is not calmness, it's empathy. – Mehmet Oz

Empathy is a skill that many boys need help to develop. Testosterone surges typically beget competition, not compassion. Learning how to respond with empathy is a valuable life skill that can be paired with another highly valuable ability: reading aloud.

This brain tip targets boys' lagging literacy skills by giving them practice reading aloud, a strategy known to support fluency. Match a boy with a younger male in a lower grade to help the older child improve receptive and expressive language by reading aloud. You can actually mix this up a bit by:

1. Having the older child read to the younger one, which encourages his capacity for empathy

OR

2. Having the older child write down the younger child's version of what was read aloud and listening as the younger child "echo reads" back the older child's words

Tip #9
Create a Book Club Just for Boys

A book club accomplishes several important tasks:

1. It gives boys a safe place to be readers.

2. It builds a sense of tribe or community.

3. It provides strong academic role models with celebrity guest readers.

4. It addresses boys' lower reading comprehension and fluency scores on standardized tests.

In spite of the enormous success of the Harry Potter series a number of years ago, an NEA study showed that boys continued to read less often than girls and that the frequency of their reading for pleasure dropped over a twenty year period.

Combat this by creating a book club just for boys, with hot cocoa "lattes"; celebrity guest readers of special interest to the students; action-packed, boy-friendly selections; and comfortable reading areas.

SECTION THREE: GIRL-FRIENDLY BRAIN TIPS

Are the differences between boys' and girls' brains significant enough to warrant two sections in this book? I think so. Remember, these differences are in style, not substance. Yet small shifts in curriculum, instruction, and assessment can make a big difference. Let's consider some initial stereotype/strategy/suggestion tips for girls:

Stereotype	Strategy	Suggestion
Girls don't do well in math.	Give girls a pep talk before a math test.	Girls "do math" from the logical and emotional brains. They need to build confidence.
Girls are too emotional.	Attach emotions to learning.	In social studies or science, target the personal impact of research or discoveries on families and communities.
Girls are afraid to be wrong, so they hesitate before making a choice.	Use more neural scaffolding. Build in wait time.	How long is "too long"? Avoid thinking in terms of competition in cognition.
Girls talk too much.	Target the talking time. Task this strength.	Configure a small group for a task, but provide a graphic organizer for girls to complete in order to focus words.

Tip #1
Use the Think, Pair, Share Model

Considering the chart at the beginning of this section, you will find that the "Think, Pair, Share" model can be ideal for girl-friendly accommodations. It works nicely because:

1. Girls use about 20,000 words per day, so they typically have plenty to say.

2. The task builds leadership and reflective skills.

3. Writing things down on the graphic organizer helps to focus thinking.

4. The "pairing" allows girls to collaborate, a favored choice.

5. It works across any area of the curriculum, but is excellent for deconstructing informational text (a Common Core emphasis).

Pair up the girls and have them read an article or piece of text. Then have them complete the graphic organizer together.

THINK	PAIR	SHARE
What was most important to you?	What did we find to be critical when we discussed it?	What do we want to tell our peers to focus on?

Tip #2
Create College and Career Collages

While working as a federal evaluator on a teen pregnancy prevention program, I stumbled on some surprising research on what keeps young girls on track for a bright future. In a tough inner-city environment where the usual high-risk behavior prevention models were floundering, something new did seem to shift girls' thinking and decision-making. And, it had nothing to do with intimacy. It had to do with investigating careers.

When the girls began sessions on career planning and college choices and thinking of themselves in a different place both literally and figuratively, they gained feelings of power and made better choices.

So, pull out the magazines and catalogs, and create "College and Career Collages," where images of women in interesting jobs are crafted into collages by the girls during "chats" on making choices. Integrate new vocabulary and real-time information about college and careers during this activity.

Tip #3
Utilize a Block Center

Adding a block center to your classroom, whether you teach kindergarten or 4th grade, is a simple, authentic way to address one of the needs of female students. You see, visual-spatial ability seems to be one of the only areas in which, at a biological level, boys and girls are not competitive from birth.

Girls' brains do seem to need more practice in acquiring fluency and flexibility in visual-spatial tasks, and blocks tend to do the trick. In one of my first published articles on brain-friendly teaching, I noted that two simple modifications increased girls' interest in and time spent using blocks and similar manipulatives:

1. Adding props, such as plastic farm animals, dinosaurs, and small dolls, enables girls' strength of "story," helping them build a narrative around a structure.

2. Separating boys and girls during block time to ensure that boys' typically aggressive moves, such as knocking over structures for no apparent reason, does not interfere with girls crafting their own structures.

Don't forget novelty and variety in girls' block choices: Lego® bricks, pattern blocks, waffle blocks, Unifix® cubes, and Tinkertoys® are all innovative and helpful in increasing depth and complexity of visual-spatial ability.

Tip #4
Give Girls Empowering Messages

In an interesting study, girls who had studied a difficult mathematics curriculum under the same instructor were then divided into two groups to review for the final examination.

In one group, the girls heard more negative messages, such as:

> *This is a very challenging test.*
> *Math is the toughest subject area.*
> *The test is going to be difficult. I hope you are prepared.*

In a separate group, the girls heard more positive messages, much like:

> *I know you are prepared for this test.*
> *You have all the skills necessary to get a great score.*
> *You girls have excelled in math and are clearly ready for the test.*

The girls who heard specific, positive, powerful messages before the test scored higher than their peers who had heard the more critical messages. The differences were significant. Why is this the case, and wouldn't it also matter to boys? It seems that estrogen makes girls more anxious, while testosterone, in the face of a challenge, makes boys more competitive. Send girls powerful messages about their competence to build their confidence.

Tip #5
Provide Worthy Role Models

Clearly, STEM (**S**cience, **T**echnology, **E**ngineering, and **M**athematics) skills are an essential focus for teachers. For girls, who for many years suffered under a mythology that females were less able in these areas, a strong commitment to STEM is critical. How can girls connect to STEM? Tap into their desire for relationships. Mentoring programs are wonderful, but tough to administer. Create historical mentors by having girls conduct research and then do interviews with the rock stars of math and science. There is an entire section on this in *Breaking Brain Barriers* (Karges-Bone 2010), complete with lists of female scientists and mathematicians.

Curie

Lucid

Hopper

Who is _____?

Where does she live and work?

Identify her major intellectual accomplishments.

Share an interesting anecdote that helps to explain her success.

Tip #6
Promote Healthy Leadership Behaviors

alpha _____

adjective
socially dominant, especially in a group of
people or animals.

Female Bully or Alpha Girl? This is a question more and more teachers grapple with. Monitor your female students for behaviors that may be harmful and destructive. This includes negative choices and patterns among strong females and the consequential impact on the Beta Girls in the group. This chart may help you discern between Alpha Girls and Budding Female Bullies.

Alpha Girl	Female Bully
Has strong opinions	Will not allow others to share their opinions
Has a wide circle of friends	Takes pleasure in moving other girls in and out of the circle
Is hard working	Assigns tasks to others instead of sharing the load
Enjoys friendships with boys and girls	May show early, aggressive sexual behavior toward males or females
Plans and creates	Plots and attacks

Tip #7
Get Girls Involved in Geography

More boys than girls compete and win in state and national geography competitions. It need not be the case. Interestingly, geography was the first physical science to be emphasized in girls' education. Check out this quote from Dr. Kim Tolley:

Some educational reformers argued that knowledge of the sciences rendered women more interesting conversationalists and companions for their husbands. According to the well-known female educator Almira Hart Lincoln Phelps, scientific study would result 'in enlarging [women's] sphere of thought, rendering them more interesting companions to men of science, and better capable of instructing the young.' Americans promoted [geography] among girls because some contemporaries perceived women as playing a key role in developing scientific interest among children. (Tolley 2003)

There are helpful hints in this excerpt. Girls typically enjoy talking, so pair that skill with tasks and materials that build geographic knowledge:

> Provide maps and atlases, both electronic and hard copies, for problem solving skills.

> Hold a monthly geography bee, and allow girls to work in pairs to study.

> Give girls the task of developing interviews with girls from other countries and take turns playing the role of interviewer and interviewee.

Tip #8
Give Girls Adequate Time to Process Mathematics

When researchers compared girls who had perfect SAT scores in mathematics with boys who scored at the same level, they found that the girls typically took longer to arrive at the answers. Is this a weakness? The answer is NO; it is an issue of style, not substance.

The *corpus callosum*, or the area that divides the left and right hemispheres of the brain, is 14 times larger in females than in males. This suggests that girls access both sides of the brain to do many skills, including math. Boys tend to do more linear thinking, going straight over to the left brain to solve math problems.

Currently, there is no statistical difference in boys' and girls' performance on math assessments, but timing issues persist in classroom instruction.

Remember
Girls like to check for accuracy.

Consider
Girls like to know how math relates to real life.

Allow
Give girls time to access left and right brain skills.

Tip #9
Teach Social Media Manners

Girls and boys love social media. It is an integral part of our culture and cannot easily be separated from school. For girls, a mini unit on social media manners can be brain friendly. Here's why:

Girls are affected by estrogen surges at a younger age, with puberty setting in as early as nine years old. Estrogen may trigger dramatic emotional responses and physical development that does not match emotional/social development. This can lead to poor choices on social media, such as bullying, "sexting" (sending sexually charged messages or images), or engaging in online relationships that can be dangerous.

What can teachers do to help girls engage in healthy social media behaviors?

Girls like to bond. Sign a pledge together as a group.

Help girls to set appropriate boundaries about images, chats, and sites.

Social Media

Involve parents in the training. Focus on monitoring online behaviors and encouraging reading and outdoor activity.

Engage in role playing and do scenarios to practice safe online skills.

SECTION FOUR: THE SENSORY BRAIN

Many school children can name the five senses, but it is doubtful that as many teachers can identify ways that ordinary items found at the grocery store can elicit powerful cognitive responses from the brain.

In this section, we will explore the "sensory brain."

Teachers can pair cognitive and sensory experiences for maximum retention and to create *episodic*, or a series of, memories. The limbic system at the back of the brain acts like the filter on a clothes dryer, capturing the lint of sensory experiences that have been presented to the brain in tandem with cognitive experiences. Involving multiple senses evokes even more cognitive payback.

Some examples:

Providing peppermints while reviewing for a test	Adding clapping to phonemic awareness activities	Practicing math facts on chilled shaving cream

Tip #1
Pop a Peppermint

Oils in the peppermint plant increase alertness by stimulating your trigeminal nerve, "which is the same nerve that's activated when you revive someone with smelling salts," says Alan Hirsch, MD, director of the Smell and Taste Treatment Foundation in Chicago. Mints also contain menthol, which makes you feel cooler and more awake.

My claim to fame is the fact that I am "the peppermint lady." In my earlier book, *Differentiated Pathways of the Brain* (Karges-Bone 2010), I tied the use of peppermint, spearmint, and wintergreen to increasing focus during high-stakes tests.

Principals can be seen at the big box stores hoarding bags of mints during the spring testing marathons. Anecdotal evidence suggests that it can be helpful, especially if students review the information while chewing on a mint and then take the test with the same scent and flavor in play.

Tip #2
Use a Metronome

Download a metronome app on your smartphone or tablet, and use it as a "brain break" to balance the two sides of the brain. (You can also use a real metronome—check with your school's music teacher or band director to see if you can borrow one.) Set it for five beats per minute, and have the students breathe slowly in and out for the full interval. This is especially helpful for boys, who need to improve their auditory focus.

This simple strategy allows for:

Focus

Clarity

Decompression

Relaxation

Centering

Tip #3
Go Green

The color green is associated cross-culturally with relaxation. Is your brain programmed green? Here are some fun facts:

It is said that green is the most restful color for the human eye.

Green has great healing power. It can soothe pain.

People who work in green environments have fewer stomach aches.

Kids who look out on "green" spaces have higher test scores.

Green is beneficial around teething infants.

Suicides dropped 34% when London's Blackfriar Bridge was painted green.

The impact of the color green on classroom tone is positive and simple to translate into neuro-architecture. Try the following:

1. Add a few green plants to the décor.

2. Paint a bookshelf green, or put green paper onto shelving.

3. Use green paper as the background on classroom
bulletin boards.

4. Use a green pen to mark papers.

5. Select green folders for student work. In one study, students whose creative writing was kept in green folders, as opposed to other colors, produced more and better prose.

Tip #4
Hide Scented Dryer Sheets

Hiding scented dryer sheets may decrease feelings of anxiety in an environment by 20%. The studies were done in homes in which dryer sheets were or were not used during laundry time, but why not make the creative leap to classrooms? Remember, scent is the strongest sense tied to memory, so we want to link positive scents to our episodic memories.

Scented dryer sheets, especially those that use scents known in medicinal circles to evoke relaxation responses, may be a nice touch. These would include lavender, chamomile, rosemary, and floral.

Where can these be hidden so as not to become distracting or interfere with allergies?

Lining waste receptacles

Cubbies

Closets and drawers

Book shelves

Cabinets under sinks and in storage areas

Tip #5
Choose Blue to Beat the Classroom Blues

Interestingly, restful shades of blue are used in mental health settings, prisons, and cardiac care units to induce feelings of cooperation and contentment. Using cardiac blue in the classroom is a well-researched strategy to reduce blood pressure, which in turn reduces feelings of stress and anxiety.

Shades of blue can be appropriate for the following purposes:

Fish tanks ⟶ **Increase relaxation**

Carpet in the story telling area ⟶ **Improve focus**

Shelf lining, border paper, paint ⟶ **Infuse soft effect**

Tip #6
Get Hands-On with Shaving Cream

Our brains operate on a continuum from sleeping or rest to a high level of alertness or wakefulness. In the classroom, especially when teachers desire a high level of attention during periods of sustained practice, a multi-sensory experience is ideal!

The use of chilled, menthol-scented shaving cream as a sensory teaching tool is inexpensive, fun, and clean! Multiple studies show that the scent of menthol is one of the more powerful neural triggers for alertness.

You will need:
1. Cans of chilled shaving cream
2. Recycled shower curtains or sheets of waxed paper
3. Rules. Lots of rules.

Practice everything from math facts to spelling words in shaving cream snow. Remember, the brain likes novelty, especially during periods of sustained practice. "Writing in the snow," especially when done outdoors, gives the brain a boost, and clean-up is a snap!

Tip #7
Use Citrus Scents in the Classroom

Brazilian scientists had participants spend five minutes inhaling one of three substances: sweet orange essential oil, tea tree oil, or plain old water. Participants then underwent a stressful test while having their vital signs measured. Those who sniffed orange oil were less anxious throughout the test, and the beneficial effects even lingered once the exam was over.

Here are some scent-sational ideas for using orange and other citrus scents in the classroom:

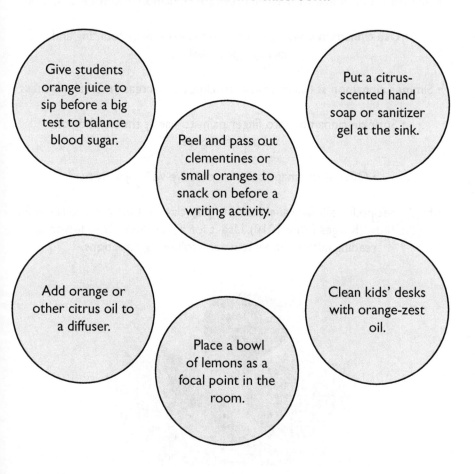

Give students orange juice to sip before a big test to balance blood sugar.

Peel and pass out clementines or small oranges to snack on before a writing activity.

Put a citrus-scented hand soap or sanitizer gel at the sink.

Add orange or other citrus oil to a diffuser.

Place a bowl of lemons as a focal point in the room.

Clean kids' desks with orange-zest oil.

Tip #8
Incorporate Cinnamon

Cinnamon is a powerful scent and flavor that can activate the brain. The scent of cinnamon can boost the brain's function. According to a 2004 study, even just smelling the scent of cinnamon has an effect on the brain's cognitive processing. The test group was subjected to different scents of cinnamon, jasmine, peppermint, and no odor. Cinnamon was shown to enhance memory, attention, recognition, and visual-motor speed.

Here are some simple ways to incorporate cinnamon into your classroom:

- Use cinnamon disks as Bingo game covers or as counting and sorting manipulatives.

- Simmer cinnamon sticks in a small crockpot to increase mental alertness.

- Sprinkle cinnamon into finger paint to use at the easel or on art paper outside.

- Offer gingersnaps before a creative writing activity.

- Find a recipe for all-natural cinnamon "play clay" in *Differentiated Pathways of the Brain* (Karges-Bone 2010). Use it for a Common Core lesson on reading informational texts and following directions.

SECTION FIVE: ACCOMMODATIONS FOR DIFFERENTIATION AND RTI

In my national workshop titled "Classroom Management ER," I tell teachers and principals two things:

1. All teachers are now special education teachers, certified in the field or not.

2. There is no such thing as normal. Normal is the setting on the clothes dryer, not in the classroom.

That may seem harsh, but it is reality as we know it today. Many students have undiagnosed mental or learning issues. In some cases, the students fall into the dreaded "gray area," that place on the assessment continuum at which it is clear that the weakness or problem exists, but is not "bad enough" to trigger a formal placement. These students will remain in regular classrooms, probably with little or no outside support. Regular classroom teachers will provide accommodations, or the more formal RTI ("Response to Intervention").

These brain-friendly accommodations are meant to add to formal IEPs or 504 plans, if they exist, or to fill in the gaps when no such plans are available. Like the section on the Sensory Brain, these strategies harness the powers of the auditory, tactile and visual modalities with a fresh approach.

Tip #1
Pick Up the Craft Sticks

Thick craft sticks are quite possibly the least expensive, most potent choices in differentiation and tiered assessment ever created. Here's why craft sticks can serve as cognitive accommodations in your classroom.

Select the pack of four different colored sticks, and assign a color to represent students' learning styles or ability levels. Of course, the students don't know this, but the teacher shifts his or her questioning strategy or task assignment to meet students' needs. The diagram below shows a suggested reference using either ability OR personality/learning style.

Color	Ability Level	Personality or Learning Style
Blue Stick	Gifted or Advanced	ADD/ADHD or Creative
Yellow Stick	Below Basic/ Struggling	Quiet/Introvert/ Analytic
Green Stick	Proficient	Compliant/Curious/ Balanced Style
Red Stick	Basic Level	Extrovert/Global Learning

Tip #2
Crank Up the Classical Music

Playing classical music is soothing and therapeutic. The "Mozart Effect," the theory that children who listen to classical music score higher on tests of reasoning, memory, and math, has been celebrated and censored for the past twenty years. Claims that strategically targeted uses of classical music enhances intelligence and performance are, at the very least, worth considering, especially when working with students who need special accommodations for:

Focus

Attention

Sustained Practice

Mood

Music is a stimulus, and we know that stimuli filter through the limbic system at the back of the brain. When paired with a cognitive experience, music may help the brain to hold onto the *schema* (knowledge about a particular concept) with greater fidelity. Classical music is very patterned and orderly, and the brain seems to respond in a unique way.

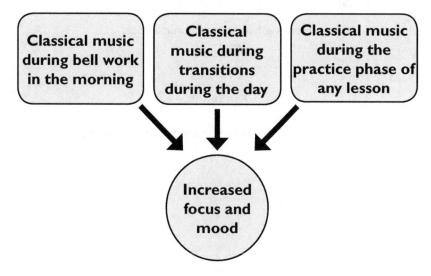

Tip #3
Apply Your Cognitive SPF

Students who struggle to learn typically struggle with memory. They cannot hold onto schema. Provide "sunscreen" for the brain with SPF.

In order to improve memory, you need three things:
1. **S**chema (organizing structure)
2. **P**ractice
3. **F**ocus

One of my students, a lifeguard at the college pool at the time, became very excited about this and said, "Dr. B, it's like sunscreen... you know, the SPF in sunscreen. Put it on every time you teach so that the lesson doesn't get burned!" She was right. For all students, but especially those who require accommodations, you must apply three steps in every lesson: 1) rich schema or knowledge, 2) lots of practice, and 3) sustained focus during the steps. Skipping a step creates cognitive dissonance, or a "pain in the brain."

Here's a handy mnemonic device:

Schema

Prevents

Forgetting

Don't forget your SPF when you are teaching new material!

Tip #4
Try Tiered Assessments and Assignments

Let them eat tiered cake!

There is learning tied to this tiered, or layered, cake. The image should be deliciously imprinted on the teacher's brain: assessments and assignments taste better when they are differentiated for students. The quintessential text on this is *How to Differentiate Instruction* (Tomlinson 1995). Author Carol Tomlinson suggests tiers to help 1) motivate and 2) differentiate struggling learners.

Some strategies:

Break assignments or assessments into two parts, given on different days. I like to do more left-brained tasks on one day and more right-brained tasks on another.

Start and end the students at different places on the assignment or assessment. Do gifted students really need to do the simple problems?

Mix in multiple intelligences, like having chocolate and vanilla flavored layers on a cake. Some students might make their vocabulary words into a poem, others into a rap or a riddle.

Tip #5
Add Clapping to Cognitive Tasks

Clapping may improve focus and help to link the left and right brain. A recent study by Ben-Gurion University suggests there is a link between clapping games and the development of important skills in both children and in young adults.

For students who struggle, creating "episodic memories" is a useful strategy, so why not add a few of these clapping opportunities into your curriculum?

• Add clapping to steps in math problems to act like Velcro® for the brain.

• Add clapping to vocabulary or spelling lessons to "imprint" the sequence of letters in the brain.

• Add clapping to transitions as students move from activity to activity.

ACCOMMODATIONS FOR DIFFERENTIATION AND RTI | 90/1096LE

Tip #6
Make the Students "Say It, Show It, Do It"

(IT is the objective.)

I was doing a series of classroom visits (58 of them, to be exact) in a site that was on the "Endangered Species List" for the state because of low test scores over a period of years. My task: to get into classrooms and see if I could identify patterns of weakness in instruction. I found some surprising things. One of the most interesting patterns was that the teachers did all of the work and the students sat back passively. The teachers asked questions and then answered them. To avoid this pitfall that occurs often when students have "learned helplessness," adopt the
SAY IT, SHOW IT, DO IT model.

In every lesson, create procedures in which the students must SAY, SHOW, and DO the objective. In this way, the teacher facilitates the mastery of the objective instead of performing it himself or herself. You need evidence, not just an experience.

Teacher Prompt	Students Give Verbal Response (SAY IT)	Students Demonstrate With a Visual Response (SHOW IT)	Students Confirm Mastery With a Correct Example (DO IT)
Pre-Assessment	As a group	Individual "clickers" or whiteboards	Small group work
Review	Individual	Identify on IWB	Pre-test

Tip #7
Take a (Brain) Break

Students who have attention, emotional, or learning problems can "overheat" very quickly. They benefit from instruction that is "chunked" into more brief experiences and "layered" with frequent practice. This is the *chunking and layering model* that I will discuss further in the Creativity and Critical Thinking section (page 63). For now, remember that everyone needs to hit the pause button about every 30 minutes. Here is a list of five favorite Brain Breaks from my workshops and books:

> An arrangement of yellow lemons in a bowl increases attention and makes a great still-life model for students to sketch as an "early finisher" task.

> Put on patriotic marching music, and have students march around for two minutes. Flag waving with mini flags is optional.

> Use a baton made from a recycled paper towel holder decorated with streamers and go outside for a "pass the math" relay.

> Play Jump the Synapse to connect learning. Go outside and chalk out a hop scotch grid, or use tape inside. Create review questions on index cards and as students respond correctly, they jump through the course. Use this for any subject area review.

> Dim the lights, and have students breathe deeply in and out of one side of the nose while gently holding the other side with a forefinger. This type of breathing balances the left and right sides of the brain.

Tip #8
Use Handwriting as a Cognitive Tool

Handwriting, especially cursive writing, seems to have implications for connecting the right and left brain, creating episodic memories, and helping with focus.

Yet scientists are discovering that learning cursive is an important tool for cognitive development, particularly in training the brain to learn "functional specialization," [2] that is capacity for optimal efficiency. In the case of learning cursive writing, the brain develops functional specialization that integrates both sensation, movement control, and thinking. Brain imaging studies reveal that multiple areas of the brain become co-activated during learning of cursive writing of pseudo-letters, as opposed to typing or just visual practice. (Klemm 2013)

These same areas of the brain are not activated during keyboarding. This is problematic, since one of the most common accommodations for students who struggle is to give them a choice not to write, but to use the keyboard.

Here are some ways you can keep handwriting as a cognitive tool:

Teach handwriting and penmanship.

Practice handwriting in small increments. Reward progress.

Allow students to use colored "rolling" pens or fat pencils to accommodate needs.

Create a publishing center where students can go to publish handwriting, even if it is simply spelling words on a list.

Tip #9
Layer the Practice

Interesting research on the brains of geniuses revealed a surprising fact. Indeed, the genius brain seems to have a head start on whatever it is that is the focus of the talent or gift. That is no surprise. What is fascinating is the fact that what seems to make us smarter is **practice**.

If a genius brain gets that way because of layers and layers of practice, then transfer that knowledge to your own classroom in which many students struggle. Practice is almost always the missing piece.

When I was tapped as a "model teacher" for special needs children a number of years ago, a team of experts literally measured (with a clicker) the number of times that I repeated, and made the students repeat, critical information and responses. My average was over 40 "clicks" per key idea.

The trick is to layer practice in novel flavors.

Spicy Practice

- Shake a maraca or ring a bell after each response.
- Clap twice and students respond once.

Sweet Practice

- Randomly toss out pieces of dark chocolate after a correct response.
- Wipe a "scenty stick" (fruity lip balm stick) on students' wrists as you review practice work.

Salty Practice

- Do a "duck, duck, goose" response model.
- Use the "Pick Up the Craft Sticks" model from this section.

SECTION SIX: NEURO-ARCHITECTURE AND THE BRAIN

When is a space more than a space? When the educator renames himself or herself as a *neuro-architect*. Educators can draw on the emerging field of neuro-architecture to create learning environments that send the right "cues" to learners.

Survey: Are You a Teacher or a Neuro-Architect?

1. I have changed the display on my door or entrance way within the last two weeks.

        YES   NO

2. Live plants and flowers play a significant role in my classroom.

        YES   NO

3. I have some kind of water, such as a fish tank or fountain, in my classroom.

        YES   NO

4. Lighting is varied in my workspace, with overhead lamps and natural lighting used in different ways.

        YES   NO

5. I have several different personalized sitting areas for students to use.

        YES   NO

6. I have built opportunities to work and play outdoors into my plans on a regular (weekly) basis.

        YES   NO

7. I like to hang and display students' work and do it in unusual ways.

        YES   NO

Did you have fewer than three YES responses? Then it's time to try something NEW!

Tip #1
Design a Brain-Friendly Classroom Space

Do not discount the importance of *social capital* on cognitive function. Briefly, students who stay connected to old and new friends experience greater verbal and creative abilities that continue through life. Be sure to create teaching and learning spaces that encourage this valuable commodity. Rows are not brain friendly. Groupings and clusters add variety, but may be more difficult to manage. Be sure your classroom management plan is set up for this kind of creative design.

Group seating in smaller, conversational ways.

Use baskets, trunks, and even an old wheel barrel as a workspace for visual appeal.

Avoid rows of seating or groups of more than four.

Define spaces into smaller, specific themes by using shower curtains, lace panels, chalkboards, or seating to create different areas.

Re-purpose unusual items for reading and writing: bean bag chairs, rocking chairs, large throw pillows, yoga mats, etc.

Change desk arrangements and group members monthly.

Tip #2
Use Natural Light

Natural sunlight is hugely important to bone growth and feelings of well-being, and yet we continue to define spaces with walls instead of natural boundaries. Moreover, research suggests that students who take "brain breaks" during study time by walking outside where they can see green spaces score higher on assessments (this is especially true for boys). Neuro-architecture with light in mind might include using some of the following items:

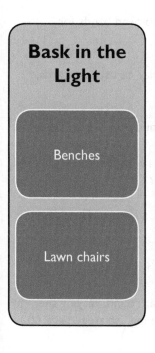

Bask in the Light

Benches

Lawn chairs

Capture the Light

Desks closer to windows

Open windows/ window boxes

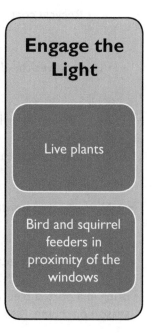

Engage the Light

Live plants

Bird and squirrel feeders in proximity of the windows

Tip #3
Draw the Eye Upward

Movement and diversity help the brain to stay focused and fertile. Build these elements into your classroom naturally by creating opportunities for students to keep looking up and around. Here are some suggestions that do double duty with organizing materials:

• Use suction cups or easy-to-remove hooks to hang a large, stained glass sun-catcher in a window, or in a blank area to "make" a window.

• Recycle coat racks to hang scarves and colored bands for movement activities.

• Use an over-the-door wreath hanger to display cards, post-cards, or greenery.

• Put up a piece of peg board, and publish poetry and artwork by students.

• Borrow the double easel from kindergarten and re-instate the art center in elementary grades.

• Add a wallpaper border with an interesting look, such as a Greek key or other geometric feature.

• Hang mobiles from the ceiling with fishing line.

• Bring in a potted tree, and hang ornaments all year round, varying them by season or theme. (See the "Create a Tree of Learning" strategy, page 60.)

Tip #4
Add Water Features to Your Classroom Environment

Jonathan Goldman, founder and director of the Sound Healers Association in Boulder Colorado, and author of the book, *Healing Sounds*, says, "The use of sound and music is the most ancient healing modality."

The sound of running water is a natural antidote to anxiety. There is a reason dentists often have elaborate aquariums in their waiting rooms. Adding a water feature, simple or fancy, is a useful way to harness the energy of neuro-architecture. The therapeutic use of water sounds is akin to music therapy, shown to reduce blood pressure, stress hormone levels, and perceptions of pain by significant amounts.

Water Features
Small fountains
Aquarium or fish bowl
Screensaver for the IWB with sights/sounds of the ocean
Murals of water and sounds on an MP3 player

Tip #5
Organize an Art Cart

A journey of a thousand miles must begin with a single step. – Lao Tzu

Neuro-architecture is an excellent first step to becoming a more brain-friendly teacher, as you set up your classroom environment to feed and nurture the brain. The brain craves several things: glucose and oxygen, of course, but also novelty, connectivity, and creativity.

Organizing an ART CART is a sure-fire way to increase cognitive and creative connectivity. Instead of planning for a separate art lesson, turn any activity into a more rich and integrated experience by wheeling out the cart. Begin with a simple, wheeled plastic cart with baskets or bins, and fill it with the following:

Scented markers

Glue sticks

Stickers

Fabric and yarn

Crayons and colored pencils

Glitter and glitter sticks

Stamps and ink pads

Other miscellaneous crafting materials

Tip #6
Name It and Frame It

As a professor who prepares future teachers, I often use children's books to make important points about cognitive science. In *The Dot*, by Peter H. Reynolds, a little girl is afraid to attempt any kind of creative work. She feels under-valued and invisible. Her teacher, a brilliant neuro-architect, encourages her to make a single dot on a piece of paper and then surprises the child by framing the work in an ornate gold frame. The outcome is nothing short of amazing. The child feels so affirmed that she ends up creating a one-girl art show.

Gather a few (plastic and gaudy) frames from a discount store or yard sale, and repurpose them for neuro-architecture. Surprise a few children each week by framing their efforts and displaying them for admiration. Don't stop with art. Frame handwriting, math quizzes, or book reports.

Let your classroom become a gallery of student creations across the curriculum.

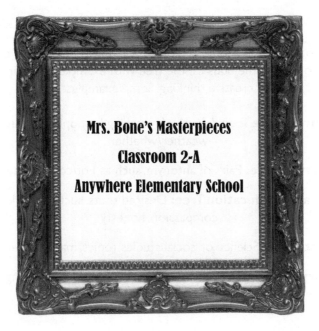

Mrs. Bone's Masterpieces

Classroom 2-A

Anywhere Elementary School

Tip #7
Create a Tree of Learning

This tip blends neuro-architecture and sensory brain research in a tangible style! Re-purpose a potted silk tree to become a "Tree of Learning" in your classroom. The branches of the tree mimic neural pathways of the brain in *dendritic arborization:*

arborization
noun 1. A branching, treelike shape or arrangement, as that of the dendrite of a nerve cell. 2. The formation of a treelike shape or arrangement.

The "Tree of Learning" should be student-driven, as in assigning or directing students to "grow" the buds on the tree with examples of their critical or creative thinking. Some examples:

Homophone Tree: Leaves of matching homophones, such as weather/whether

Antonym Tree: Pairs of antonym, such as hot/cold and new/old

Character Education Tree: Desired traits, such as work ethic, compassion, honesty

Facts Tree: Science or social studies topics, math properties

Literary Elements Tree: Plot, point of view, conflict, setting, theme

Tip #8
Readopt Learning Centers

I spent a year teaching kindergarten in an at-risk school on a huge military base. My faithful assistant Miss Carol and I had 32 children in the AM session and 32 again after lunch. That is 64 different children, many of whom had language delays, were from other countries, or came from large, complex families where one parent was deployed for six months at a time. Wild! I tell you, without our "centers," all would have been lost. Unfortunately, most elementary classrooms morph into sterile environments shortly after first grade.

But re-think the neuro-architecture. You can adopt the center as a model for more sophisticated curricula. Centers are brain-friendly because they allow learning styles and multiple intelligences to flourish. Centers create interest, manage movement, and use space in effective ways.

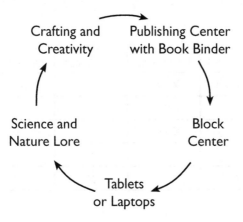

Crafting and Creativity → Publishing Center with Book Binder

Science and Nature Lore

Block Center

Tablets or Laptops

Just be sure to mix up the holdings in the centers. For example:

1. The "water" center sometimes has bubbles and other times it has floating objects.
2. The art center might have paint, or it might have materials to make note cards with pressed flowers.
3. The fine motor center might have wooden puzzles or a beading craft.
4. The publishing center morphs according to holidays and seasons.

Tip #9:
Get Colorful

The brain responds to color in unique and powerful ways. The teacher acting as a practicing neuro-architect takes advantage of the therapeutic use of color for purposes including:

Printing tests
Backgrounds on bulletin boards
Notes to parents
Rugs and lamp shades
Creating games and worksheets
Grading work

The "Brain-Bow" chart below suggests some innovative ways to match color and classroom.

	Excitement	Creativity	Alertness	Reflection	Relaxation
Blue	X Royal	X Sky		X Aqua	X Teal
Brown		X			X Creamy
Green	X Lime	X Jade		X	X Melon
Purple			X		
Orange	X	X	X		

SECTION SEVEN: CREATIVITY AND CRITICAL THINKING

Research suggests that students in the US are becoming "less creative." Scores on IQ tests have inched higher, while scores on assessments of creativity have been declining for more than a decade.

We need an innovation infusion!

Creativity and critical thinking are treated collaboratively in this section. These strategies challenge teachers and students to move beyond the ordinary and explore the possibilities of more elaborate and refined thinking. All students benefit from more creative and critical thinking tasks, but some demand it. There are times when classroom management issues are actually rooted in boredom or restlessness. These terms come to mind:

Wild children

Divergent thinkers

Sensitive

Verbal

Advanced

Intelligent

Critical thinkers

Problem solvers

Innovators

Curious

You need **innovation** in your thinking!

Tip #1
Lay a Creative Egg

Both creativity and critical thinking feed on novelty. There is actually a neural basis for "sensation seeking" in the brain. (Patoine 2009)

Dopamine is triggered when students encounter novel or fresh classroom experiences. That is a desired outcome. So trigger more dopamine by using inexpensive, colorful plastic eggs.

Activity	Critical Thinking	Creative Thinking
Review for a test by putting "clues," such as page numbers or key vocabulary, in an egg and having students search out the evidence in the textbook.	X	
Hide math problems in eggs around the room, and have students find and solve them on a worksheet or whiteboard.		X
After reading a story, nest examples of the literary elements, such as setting, point of view, plot, and conflict, in eggs and toss them out to students to identify.	X	X

Tip #2
Provide White Space

Every child is an artist. The problem is how to remain an artist once we grow up.
– Pablo Picasso

One of the most simple, yet effective, strategies is also the most difficult to implement. It is called white space. *White space* is a technical term for providing planned but unstructured time for the brain to decompress and re-align. It is essential for creative thinking.

If you want students to be more creative, you must give them time to do
NOTHING.

This flies in the face of all we know about "losing instructional time." But if you study the most successful organizations, the use of white space becomes immediately clear. Set up a tub of white space props, and give students "tickets" for five minutes of time to:

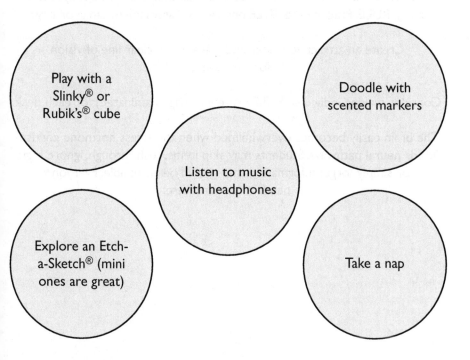

Play with a Slinky® or Rubik's® cube

Doodle with scented markers

Listen to music with headphones

Explore an Etch-a-Sketch® (mini ones are great)

Take a nap

Tip #3
Follow the RULE for Responses

Students who are test wise can outperform students of equal ability but lacking test-wiseness. — Thomas Scruggs & Margo Mastropieri

Critical thinking doesn't just happen. It has RULES.

R	Read the question two times.
U	Underline the question.
L	Listen as you say the question to yourself.
E	Examine the question for critical words.

Train your students to become more critical thinkers with a simple test-taking RULE. Practice the RULE before each assessment, small or large.

Create an attractive poster, and place it in a clear line of vision for all students.

Consider making individual RULE sentence strips (laminated) for each desk.

The brain easily becomes overwhelmed when the stress hormone cortisol floods neural pathways. Students may skip items, rush through, ignore logic, or simply forget information that should be accessible. Everyone needs more structure.

Tip #4
"Overnight It to Me"

One of my favorite critical and creative thinking activities is often used in organizations known for innovation. It is linked to the research on motivation.

Once a quarter, on Thursday afternoons, it (the company) says to its software developers: "Go work on anything you want. Do it the way you want. Do it with whoever you want. Only thing we ask is that you show what you created to the rest of the company on Friday afternoon" - in this kind of fun, freewheeling, Friday afternoon meeting. It calls these things "FedEx days," because you have to deliver something overnight. (Pink 2009)

Students need three things for critical thinking: autonomy, master, and purpose. This activity, derived from Daniel Pink's book *Drive: The Surprising Truth About What Motivates Us* gives them all three!

1. Break students into small groups.

2. Assign a general topic, linked to something that you have been studying, so that they have adequate schema.

3. Give out empty (recycled) overnight mailing envelopes.

4. Challenge them to come up with a fresh way of thinking about the topic and seal it in the envelope.

5. Have students share their ideas with the class.

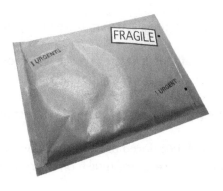

Tip #5
Talk Less and Ask Prompting Questions

The scientist is not a person who gives the right answers, he's one who asks the right questions. – Claude Lévi-Strauss

Teachers talk too much. In fact, we call this "over-talking" in the literature. It is especially threatening to male students, who may become overwhelmed when female teachers rely too much on the auditory modality.

So use your words carefully, and use them to encourage more creative and critical thinking.

Develop a set of prompting questions that generate meaningful responses.

Critical Thinking
Is there another way to think about that?
What evidence do you find for your answer?

Creative Thinking
How could you make this more unique?
What might happen if you changed things slightly?

Motivation
Can you imagine another answer?
Are you excited about the way this is turning out?

Post the prompts around the classroom to remind you and the students.

Use the Pick Up the Craft Sticks strategy (page 44) to broaden the reach of your questions.

Toss a Question Ball (page 15) to involve kinesthetic learning.

Outline a question mark in colored tape on the floor, and make it a friendly "stage" for responses, a fresh take on neuro-architecture.

Tip #6
Swipe "Scenty" Sticks

Scent is a reliable trigger for creativity. When inexpensive "scenty" sticks, so named by a creative kindergarten teacher who shared this idea at a workshop, are used as a classroom management tool, the possibilities are sweet indeed!

Here's the trick: swipe a scented lip balm on students' up-turned wrists so that they can "sniff and study" while working. Simply use the proximity method and work the room checking for accuracy and progress while students are doing seat or group work. Train the children to hold their wrists up if they want a dab of the daily scent. Put the Scent of the Day on the board each morning as an incentive!

Scent is the strongest sense tied to memory. The limbic system and reticular activating device are in play, creating episodic memories. Pleasant scents also help to increase serotonin and dopamine levels, thereby enhancing mood. Fruity scents are associated with creative thinking. Minty or woodsy scents trigger alertness. Cinnamon and ginger do both!

Tip #7
Give Graphology Exercises

American school children often stumble over the critical thinking task of extracting information and data from charts, graphs, and text. If the answer is right in front of them, students are fine, but embed the answer in a feature such as a graph and it might as well be in Latin!

To improve critical thinking, give the brain a twice-weekly "graphology" exercise. It does for the cerebrum what Pilates does for the core.

Graphology Tips:

Examine graphs from magazines or newspapers on the document camera.

Make graphs once a week using student-driven data.

Vary the styles of graphs—chart, pie, bar, etc.

Do a graphology scavenger hunt with teams hunting answers that require graphs.

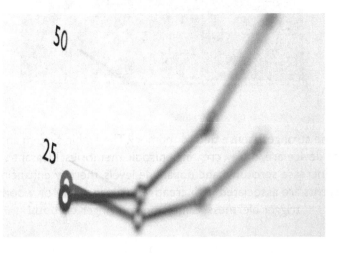

Tip #8
Tabletop Texting

By the time they are 14 years old, boys are sending over 30 texts per day, and girls? Over 100. That's a lot of language! But are teachers getting any benefit? I think not. Let's turn the tables with some tabletop texting!

There is no technology involved—just chart paper or whiteboards and colored markers (scented, if possible). This is ideal for working on informational texts in science or social studies.

Assign small groups of students a chunk of text in the textbook, markers, and a medium for recording key information. This is good for the review stage of the learning cycle, before an assessment.

Students read and review the chunk and then pass the text around the table, adding key information. They should respond to what has already been "texted." Here's an example created from a 4-5 page excerpt from a science book:

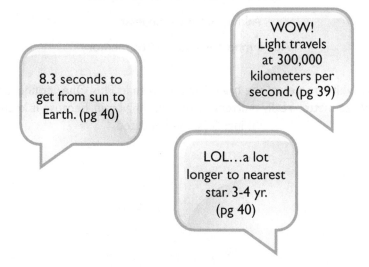

Students should give page numbers for evidence, because these texts will be posted to be used as study tools for the entire class.

Tip #9
Consider Brain-Friendly Practices to Be Your "Plus One"

White matter is one of the two components of the central nervous system. It consists mostly of axons and support cells that transmit signals from one region of the brain to another.

Keeping the white matter busy and engaged requires constant attention. The brain looks for novelty and connectivity. Studies suggest that our brains function at a more productive level after practicing creative and stimulating activities, such as acting, drama, or juggling. Of course, teachers cannot add entire chunks to the day. But perhaps there is time for a quick addition of brain-friendly creativity, a "Plus One" to your classroom RSVP:

Add scented markers to record the sequence of events.

Add neon-colored sticky notes to mark critical text.

Add a "T Chart" or Venn diagram.

Add a rhyme to the lesson.

Add a mnemonic device for memory.

The white matter of the brain benefits from a "Plus One" connection. White matter really matters to the growing brain, because it keeps things fresh and updated.

SECTION EIGHT: PARENTING WITH THE BRAIN IN MIND

Is it possible to raise smarter children? The answer is …yes.

Ten deceptively simple strategies connect neurons and beget new neurons. When taken collectively and layered over time, these choices affect the health of the brain and the entire family.

1. Early bedtime helps the brain to grow and memory to take hold.

2. Water hydrates neural connections.

3. Eating fish three times per week feeds brains and raises grades.

4. The more books in the home, the smarter the child.

5. Classical music and music lessons play a premium in brain development.

6. Smart kids have smart toys, not smart phones. Toys that feed creativity are a must.

7. Outdoor play and sports increase brain capacity.

8. Talking with children, not at children, grows brains and builds trust.

9. Aim for the most colorful meals possible to use foods as brain tonics.

10. Monitor stress levels and keep an orderly home.

Making these choices in the home increases *neural plasticity*, or the ability of the brain to reorganize neural connections as a result of learning new things.

Tip #1
Give the Growing Brain the Sleep It Craves

This is the first tip, because it is so primal and practical. Research suggests that 1) the brain cleans and renews connections during sleep, 2) the hippocampus records information into long-term memory during deep sleep, and 3) many children do not get enough sleep. Lack of sleep impacts learning, mood, and memory.

Studies suggest that parents are too lax with bedtime routines. Parents need to control bedtime! ADHD may be mis-diagnosed when fatigue and sleep problems are the real culprit.

A study of 10,000 children from University College London revealed a clear clinical and statistically significant link between bedtimes and behavior. The researchers say irregular bedtimes affected children's behavior by disrupting their bodies' natural rhythms, leading to sleep deprivation that affects the developing brain. (Kelly, Kelly and Sacker 2013)

The moral of the story? Put children to bed early and consistently.

Tip #2
Hydrate the Brain

Sodas and sugary juices are not brain friendly; the brain needs WATER! The brain is 85% water. A mere 2% drop in hydration affects memory and focus.

The link between hydration and thinking is quite simple. Neural connections "jump" across synapses in the brain with the energy of an electrical charge. Water is a conductor of electricity, triggering the circuitry of the brain. Many children who do not get enough water may become sluggish for this reason.

- Give each child a water bottle and fill it daily. Make sure it is BPA-free.

- Serve water in clear pitchers at meals. Let children wash and cut lemons and cucumber slices to add to the water.

- Let children keep a water chart and track their consumption as a math task. Graph it weekly.

- Avoid drink mixes that contain red and orange food dyes. These are associated with triggering ADHD.

- Consider green tea (hot or cold) as an alternative. Green tea contains powerful, brain-friendly antioxidants.

Tip #3
Eat More Fish

Eating more fish is a good choice for parents who want their children's brains to be as healthy as possible. Studies suggest that children who consume more fish have higher grades. Eating fish may help improve critical thinking performance and focus.

In an Oxford University study of 500 children, those who had higher levels of omega-3 fatty acids were significantly more likely to score better on reading and memory tests and had fewer behavioral problems. (Richardson, et al. 2012)

Start fishing for smarter kids!

Switch out meat for fish at least three times per week.

Consider fish oil supplements.

Why not have a "fish night" each week? Make it super brain-friendly and go technology-free that same night.

Tip #4
Create a Literacy-Rich Home

From the book *Freakonomics* (Levitt and Dubner 2009):
The number of books in the home correlates to children's school success. The most successful way to improve the reading achievement of low-income children is to increase their access to print.

Findings show higher-than-average scores among students who reported more types of reading material at home. (Donahue, et al. 2001)

The brain needs BOOKS AND WORDS! Kids who come from literacy-rich homes have higher grades and are more likely to be successful. You can easily make your home a literacy-rich environment:

- Buy books for holiday and birthday gifts.
- Get a library card and visit often.
- Look for books at dollar and discount stores.
- Follow book series.
- Develop favorite authors.
- Set up a library at home.
- Try the "Tumble Books" app that reads to your child from a tablet or eReader.

Tip #5
Make Beautiful Brain Music Together

Musical training is associated with stronger verbal memory. Participating in band or choir is associated with higher grades and graduation rates. Kids who "do music" also do better on college-entrance exams such as the SAT.

New research from Northwestern University, however, suggests that musical experience offers more than just a boost in the classroom. Just a few years of music education in childhood seems to have long-term effects, including the reversal of some age-related auditory decline.

The research is impressive. Music makes the mind more flexible and strong. Incorporate music into your daily routine when possible, including playing tapes or CDs of classical music in the car and in the home.

Tip #6
Smart Kids Have Smart Toys, Not Smart Phones

On my radio program "Prayerful Parenting," I give one-minute nuggets of advice about brain-based, spiritually uplifting family time. A recent message got a lot of pushback. I described a young family seated across from me at a restaurant: mom, dad, and two little ones of preschool age. All four of them were glued to their devices for most of the meal, seldom engaging in conversation except to correct the children about how and what to eat. I thought it was sad.

Smart children need smart toys and the undivided attention of adults. Although electronics can be electrifying for the brain, they also "do all the work" for children. Be sure that your children have a balance of media and meaning in their toys. Schedule regular "unplugged" time.

High Creativity
Art and Crafting Materials
Different Kinds of Blocks

High Motion
Bubbles and Water Toys
Balls and Hoops

High Touch
Puppets and Props for Drama
Clay and Mixed Media

Tip #7
Participate in Outdoor Brain Play

Outdoor play and vigorous movement actually increase the capacity and complexity of children's brains, by triggering the release of BDNF. BDNF, or *brain-derived neurotrophic factor,* acts like Miracle Gro® for the brain. It connects neurons as well as stimulates the formation of new ones.

Active children also benefit from exercise-induced neurogenesis. A Columbia University study in 2007 showed that the *dentate gyrus,* a part of the hippocampus, demonstrated a 2- to 3-fold increases in the rate of neurons "birthed" with structured exercise.

Tip #8
Talk With Children, Not at Them

The brain needs "attachment" in the form of conversations, connections, collaboration, cooperation, and consideration of feelings. Moreover, the most significant factor in early learning is the sheer number of words children hear during the first three years of life. Words build brains.

ASK	about children's experiences, feelings, observations.
PRACTICE	active listening, a strategy of carefully listening and then re-stating what the child says.
USE	"I statements" rather than accusatory "You statements" to give feedback.
SCHEDULE	quiet times to talk about ordinary things.
GIVE	children permission to disagree in a respectful way.
MODEL	polite, polished speech and language patterns.
MAKE	words, books, and language a valuable commodity in your home.

Tip #9:
Prepare Colorful Meals to Feed Complex Brains

The more colorful the meal, eaten together, the more anti-oxidants available to the hungry young brain. As a general rule, the darker and richer the color, the more vitamin packed. Some top brain foods for your family:

Almonds
Beans
Blueberries
Dark Chocolate
Eggs
Greens
Kale
Salmon
Spinach
Tuna

Following this advice, your child may be 35% less likely to engage in disordered eating, 24% more likely to eat healthier foods, and 12% less likely to be overweight. (Hammons and Fiese 2011)

Eating meals together and making those meals brain-friendly can change the brains of both adults and children.

At your next parent-teacher workshop, create door-prizes of "Brain Food" baskets to encourage healthy families.

Tip #10
Reduce Stress and Clutter in the Home

Clutter in the home creates a "messy brain" so much so that children who live in cluttered homes earn fewer A grades than peers who live in more organized abodes. Reduce clutter, and provide a neat, quiet space for studying and reading.

Stress stops the brain from developing normally. There is an almond-shaped gland deep in the brain, called the *amygdala*. It deals with emotional learning. Fear, anxiety, and stress "turn it on," and once it is on, it may be days, weeks, or longer before it turns off. The brain is in survival mode during this time and does not function normally.

Strive to make your home:
Neat
Welcoming
Orderly
Literacy-Rich

REFERENCES

Cherniss, Cary. 1995. *Beyond Burnout: Helping Teachers, Nurses, Therapists and Lawyers Recover From Stress and Disillusionment.* New York: Routledge.

Danielson, Charlotte. 1996. *Enhancing Professional Practice: A Framework for Teaching.* Alexandria: Association for Supervision and Curriculum Development (ASCD).

Donahue, Patricia L, Robert J Finnegan, Anthony D Lutkus, Nancy L Allen, and Jay R Campbell. 2001. "The Nation's Report Card, 4th Grade Reading, 2000." *National Center for Education Statistics* . April. Accessed December 30, 2013. http://nces.ed.gov/nationsreportcard/pdf/main2000/2001499.pdf.

Edelman, Gerald M. 1992. *Bright Air, Brilliant Fire: On the Matter of the Mind.* New York: BasicBooks.

Elmore, Tim. 2010. *Habitudes: The Art of Self-Leadership.* Atlanta: Poet Gardener Publishing.

Hammons, Amber J, and Barbara H Fiese. 2011. "Is Frequency of Shared Family Meals Related to the Nutritional Health of Children and Adolescents?" *Pediatrics.* February 4. Accessed December 30, 2013. http://pediatrics.aappublications.org/content/127/6/e1565.full.

Karges-Bone, Linda. 2010. *Breaking Brain Barriers.* Dayton: Lorenz Educational Press.

—. 2010. *Differentiated Pathways of the Brain.* Dayton: Lorenz Educational Press.

Kelly, Yvonne, John Kelly, and Amanda Sacker. 2013. "Changes in Bedtime Schedules and Behavioral Difficulties in 7 Year Old Children." *Pediatrics.* October 21. Accessed December 30, 2013. http://pediatrics.aappublications.org/content/early/2013/10/09/peds.2013-1906.abstract?sid=9f9aeb7d-4dcb-44fa-9b6f-3b42eee97e65.

Klemm, William. 2013. "What Learning Cursive Does for Your Brain." *Psychology Today,* March 14.

Levitt, Steven D, and Stephen J Dubner. 2009. *Freakonomics: A Rogue Economist Explores the Hidden Side of Everything.* New York: HarperCollins.

Patoine, Brenda. 2009. "Desperately Seeking Sensation: Fear, Reward, and the Human Need for Novelty." *The Dana Foundation.* October. Accessed December 30, 2013. https://www.dana.org/media/detail.aspx?id=23620.

Pink, Daniel H. 2009. *Drive: The Surprising Truth About What Motivates Us.* New York: Riverhead Books.

Richardson, Alexandra J, Jennifer R Burton, Richard P Sewell, Thees F Spreckelsen, and Paul Montgomery. 2012. "Docosahexaenoic Acid for Reading, Cognition and Behavior in Children Aged 7–9 Years: A Randomized, Controlled Trial (The DOLAB Study)." *PLOS One.* September 6. Accessed December 30, 2013. http://www.plosone.org/article/info%3Adoi%2F10.1371%2Fjournal.pone.0043909.

Tolley, Kim. 2003. *The Science Education of American Girls.* London: RoutledgeFalmer.

Tomlinson, Carol Ann. 1995. *How to Differentiate Instruction in Mixed-Ability Classrooms.* Alexandria: Association for Supervision & Curriculum Development.